The Little Book of Scattered Thoughts

Susannah Cord

WILLIAM COLLINS

Susannah Cord

Susannah Cord was raised in Denmark, Kenya and Zimbabwe. Susannah is a lifelong horsewoman, writer and aspiring nature photographer. She was a longtime contributor to online global publication, Horses For LIFE Magazine, with her popular column, Riding By Torchlight. Susannah is the author of illustrated children's book, 'Fenella, A Fable of a Fairy Afraid to Fly' and the blog 'The Torchlight Chronicles' where she writes about life, horses and everything in between. Other Susannah Cord books include 'Tips for Expectant Writers,' 'Seeds of Change' and a forthcoming novel to be announced soon. As a devoted dressage rider and trainer, Susannah on occasion rides for the Foundation for Classical Horsemanship. Susannah lives on a horse farm in Texas with her husband Alex and what is generally acknowledged as too many horses, dogs, cats and donkeys.

About This Book

This brand new book from Susannah Cord documents blog articles from her blog "The Torchlight Chronicles." All of these articles have been previously published and are available to subscribers of the blog.

Sand Castles

So, I am about to take off for a week again, but thought I'd leave you with something. I took this picture, kind of liked it and was playing around with something to write about it. Then, in the far recesses of my mind, a memory stirred, and it seemed to me I once wrote something called Sand Castles. Lo and behold, I went straight to the right old journal (I mean, we are talking decades here) and found it on my first try. So here you go. From a very young, work-in-progress me... to you. It's kinda sweet...

Sand Castles

I built us a castle

of the finest sand my love could find

I made it our kingdom

our paradise, our refuge

We were king and queen
Untouchable
Nothing could come between
you and I.

Monsters, demons and devils
they all passed our way
our castle held strong
weathered every gale
withstood every storm
We didn't have much
but for a spell
it was enough.

We lived each day as a fairy tale
Cocooned in a shell
of gilded dreams
our love the finest pearl
or so I thought

Susannah Cord

For Time has a funny way

of changing the face of life

And what one day

seems so real

The next

can seem the strangest dream.

So it is

my fine castle

vanished before my eyes

In the single swell

of an oncoming tide.

As I sat and watched

helpless to the change

A sweet voice

whispered in my ear.....

It was just a sandcastle,

no more

no less real

Than your past and your future

Reality is now

It is here.

The Surrender

Nobody gets up in the morning expecting a tragedy. You're just up, minding your own business—having breakfast, packing your bags, writing your list and checking it twice, walking the dog, getting the kids off to school and yourself off to work—and yet it happens, every day. Every minute of every day, a tragedy is taking place somewhere, somehow, in somebody's life. One minute you're living your life as it exists, then and now, and the next you're holding an empty bag, your life shattered on the sidewalk, wondering how you will ever pick up all those itsy bitsy pieces and pretend they make up a life. Your life. Because nothing can ever be the same; nothing will ever fit quite as it did before.

How can people be scurrying by you as if nothing has happened, as if the world goes on as before? Do they not see the tangled debris on the pavement that used to be everything you had, everything that made up your life? Don't they care?

Your life that felt so real and solid and *important* somehow, exposed as nothing more than a fragile house of mirrors. You are left with a naked truth only you can know, only you can face. A lesson only you can comprehend. The last mirror left standing in a pile of shards, and it's you.

Maybe you're angry. Maybe you're in too much pain to find the strength to be angry. Maybe you're numb and the shock is insulating you from all the horror - for the moment. Maybe you're just too tired to move, and all you want to do is close your eyes and never, ever open them again.

Perhaps you have moments of surging pride and strength where you stand tall and shake your fists at the heavens and declare that tomorrow is another day and the powers that be will not get the better of you. Yet, in the next moment you may find yourself on your knees begging for their mercy, begging for respite from the pain that shreds your soul. You're curled up in a ball like a budding foetus with your ear pressed to the ground, searching for a heartbeat, any heartbeat, any sign that you are not as alone as you feel.

However you get there, however long it takes, the day will come when you find the key to your pain and you know you are not alone, never were. And regardless of who, what, how and why, it is always the same. It is the moment when you stop fighting the facts, stop charging at windmills.

The key is the surrender, the understanding that you will never understand, that this must be released to the heavens like a thousand fluttering white doves, to wing their way to freedom and carry you to peace. It is the surrender that washes away the agony and leaves in its place a muted throb, almost a heartbeat, a soft pink scar where a gaping wound once stood and screamed of the travesty committed against you.

The surrender is the miracle you thought would never be, that brings life where you had thought a desert. The surrender is the key that opens a door you thought had been locked for good, the key that sets your heart to beating once more. Not like before, perhaps, for what is done is done. No, not like before. But full again once more, rich with what was and full of what may now become.

The Little Book of Scattered Thoughts

Jacob's Widow

So in my last blog I promised you something totally different, and here it is. This is a piece I wrote many years ago, inspired by some little thing I saw on TV that grew into a sudden outpouring of this woman's story as if I was possessed by her ghost. God knows I was way too young to relate to her suffering and dreams, yet I felt every nuance of her story as if it was my own. I hope I managed to do her justice. You will be the judge.

Jacob's Widow

I am yet

a woman

My breasts mold softly, firmly

to my chest

My hips flare under this

dust drenched dress

And sometimes, late in these

deserted nights

I dream

and awake sighing

to the curving of my flesh

I am yet

a woman

although at times

I do question this belief

My hands knead dirt and dough

with like determination as

flour and dust mingle

in stripes of warpaint on my face

My children laugh

I laugh with them

Susannah Cord

They are my will, my joy, my respite

Jacob.

What guise of fate met him on the trail

to Buffalo's Gate

Three years now, a mountain a piece

I watched him ride away

through windhassled sheets of sleet

He was good

Jacob

Salt of the earth, I whispered

to the creases of his tanned neck

when we lay close

as my mothers silver spoons

in their velvet bed

Jacob chuckled then

always

between deepening breaths of sleep

and pulled my arms tighter

around his chest

his breaths slow and deep

He would have come back

were he

alive

with or without the bull and heifers

around which we thought to ply our lives

He was a good man

and I

was a good wife

At times I dream

with my eyes open wide

I dream of a man

Susannah Cord

of his roughhewn hands

Sometimes he wears a face

like Jacob's

blond and broad and tanned

and I -

am his good wife

Sometimes he wears the face of a stranger

slanted steel gray eyes resting

in glittering danger

over curving cheekbones

in a countenance

marked, enhanced

by the wilderness

that surrounds us in our naked dance

And I am no longer - Jacob's good wife

A dream alone, he is not, this stranger

I saw him once

spare and rawboned

astride his rustic pony

rolling a cigarette

at the edge of a field, freshly sown

by which we passed

on our way

to the unknown

A trembling passed through me

under his peruse

I felt no longer

fumbling

towards

womanhood

with innocence yet to lose

I was there

a woman's heart pumped

Susannah Cord

Venus blood

through aching breasts and loins

Then flushed my face with shame

and internal strife

for I was newly

Jacob's good wife

I am yet a woman

the young girl long outgrown

as children outgrew

my womb

Two now

in the ground

two still safe and sound

they have Jacob's good heart

strong body and fair hair

but in their faces,

I claim the lion's share

In the boy
I see my father
gentled by the innocence
of youth

Yet firm as his
in determination to be a man
fight nail and tooth
hand over hand

The girl-
she is all mine, as I was
before this ponderous demise

Dark arching brows
over almond hazel eyes
aquiline nose

Susannah Cord

fine and freckled by the sun

smooth skin browned

around lips rich as ripe plums

Her smile aches in my bones

so sheer

and unlined

A robustness there

no longer reflected

in mine

My sweat soaks this earth

that feeds me

at a price

I am still young

am I not?

Jacob's Widow

the words stall, sour, in my throat

startles me, urges me to flee

Such antiquity

they seem

to lay over me

At night

I walk under a stardusted sky

it lifts above me

farther and farther

rising with the exultant cry

of my heart

I watch with the wind

drawing grim tears

stinging my teeth

whipping my hair

Banishing the years

I feel life

Susannah Cord

well up in me

like a woman stirring

from a deep sleep

to her lovers touch

I am yet a woman

I remain unspayed

by this unforgiving labour

Alone though I am

with my children and my soil

This flesh slowly hardening on my bones

And to Jacob

the wilderness holds me

relentlessly loyal

In the harsh night wind

I sense the slant-eyed rider

I tie wishes to tumbleweeds

with bright ribbons of hope

That he may find them in his travels

and know

I am waiting

waiting

For I am yet a woman

awaiting plucking by hungry hands and mouth

I hang full and ripe from this twisted vine

that is my life

And life flows, back and forth, surges

between myself and this meter of Time

But in the whitewashed glare of day

I feel the scales tip

and not

in my favour

I watch my fullness shrivel

drying in the sun

Susannah Cord

my lips pale and cracked

where they, too, once

wore the richness of plums

Such days, I sense with relief the

falling of the night

wherein I may reclaim, under its cover

its swelling sky and cruel winds

that, around which in daylight

I dare only hover

In its void

I am anywhere, anytime, anything

I am woman

all softly clinging shapes

of half and full moons

aglow with the tingle of anticipation

of a lover expecting a lover soon

I am no more

Jacob's good wife

There is no Jacob to whom to be good

I am Jacob's widow

and the dry, raspy loneliness

of those insipid words

cover me like a tepid dust

from which I awake choking

my dreams cracked and broken

my bones hard and poking

under toughened skin

I am Jacob's Widow

I am a woman yet

Still, I awake sighing

to the curving

of my flesh.

So Long, Old Friend, So Long

I put a treasured friend to rest today. If old rules of thumb hold true, he was well over a hundred years old. You may be guessing my old friend was a dog, and you'd be right. But he wasn't just any old dog. He was my constant blessing for over sixteen years and as my husband likes to say - this dog was a one in a million. Of course he was. He was my boy!

When I was but a wee little girl, someone, probably my parents, gave me a floppy toy dog. I loved him dearly and well above all my other beloved toy pets, and for some strange and inexplicable reason, I named my stuffed toy Chico. Where a tow headed, blue eyed little Danish girl living in Danish suburbia came up with a Spanish word like Chico, nobody knows, least of all me. I don't even remember receiving the dog, I was so little, but I remember loving him for years and years, no matter how tattered and matted and worn he became.

Years later I was a twenty something year old woman living fancy free and footloose, travelling the country in an old Ford Econoline cargo van. I worked odd jobs at Renaissance fairs, never knowing where I was headed next, or if I'd have the money to get me there. I loved every second of it, the freedom, the leaps of faith, the solitude on long drives.

I was between fairs, visiting my dear friend Tracy. Sipping wine on the front porch of the home she shared with three other girls and two big dogs, we were commiserating over our useless love lives when the dogs went berserk at the back door. There on the back step, with only a screen door between him and two big dogs barking and growling ferociously, sat a calm puppy gazing up at us with warm amber eyes lined in kohl, all smiles and politely wagging tail.

Ignoring the dogs, he turned his little white and brindle head and looked directly at me as if to say: "I have arrived. Please adjust accordingly."

Tracy laughed and said "I think you just got yourself a dog!" I denied and denied. She reminded me I had often said I'd like a dog. I had no recollection of ever saying any such thing. My lifestyle allowed for *no such thing*. By his condition it was clear he was a stray but we made the usual rounds to no avail. Nobody knew him.

But I never knew where I was headed, never mind if they allowed dogs. No dog for me.

But I did allow we should bring him in and give him a bath and feed him and so on. He politely put up with it all, but if I moved, he moved. An hour later when I walked out behind the house to fetch something from the van, I stopped dead in my tracks when I heard an awful yelping and yapping. Seconds later came a little bundle of flapping ears and tongue and tail, tearing down the driveway to my side, where he sat down and wagged his tail happily as if to say "I thought you left without me! But I was wrong, wasn't I?"

Yes, he was wrong, and I just got myself a dog. When thinking of names, Tracy, her mind as always much quicker than mine, began reeling off names at the speed of a livestock auctioneer. "Fido, Mickey, Wooffie, Waldo, Chico, Lassie, Puppy, Fred, George, Fluffy, Bingo....." Wait, I cried! Did you just say *CHICO*?! And so it was my stuffed toy dog came to life and was the best living, breathing, walking, talking dog ever.

I always joked that Chico should have been a guy's dog - after all, he was a bona fide 'chick magnet'. I couldn't walk him anywhere without adoring crowds of girls and women fawning over him. All the more amusing, as he rarely let them touch him. He was a one woman kind of dog, and he didn't much care for men. It took my boyfriend-future-husband months to get on petting terms with Chico, but then they remained firm friends. Most people did not have that luck. Chico would put on his polite and friendly front, the smile and the slowly wagging tail, even sniff their hand, but should they move to pet him he'd flinch away and look at them with indignance, his meaning clear: "I didn't say you could TOUCH me."

They loved him anyway. He was the kind of dog everyone in the neighbourhood knew, even if they didn't know me. One day I was walking him through the equestrian center where I worked and as a woman approached, I happened to call Chico to my side. "Oh!" she called to me with a friendly grin, "Are you with Chico?" Oh yes, said I, and proudly. I'm with Chico. He acquired me some time ago.

Nobody knew what Chico was though everyone wanted to know. He looked like something different to everyone. A Corgi in a Jack Russell suit. A Jack Russell in an oversized dachshund body with the paws of a mastiff. A PBGV with short ears (yeah, I had to look that one up too). Finally I wearied of the endless discussions and opinions. If anyone asked what he was, I simply said: "He's a *GOOD* dog." And he was. He was always just perfect, with a sixth sense of what circumstance required of him. He was a gentleman.

If I was feeling mischievous, I'd say: "He's a French Roadrunner." When the listener looked puzzled, I'd follow up with: "Also known as a Louisiana

Shrimper, or colloquially as a Cajun Swampdog."
That usually did it. Chico and I would exchange
conspiratorial glances and be on our way.

I considered having him DNA tested. But somehow
that would have spoiled the fun and dampened his
air of mystery. I left his ancestry to his ancestors and
Chico to his own unique self.

In his last years, I began to take him to the groomers
for a wash and then after a year of baths, we added a
haircut. I had done the honours myself for years on
the bathing, but now I had a second dog who
required serious grooming and it was just easier.
Besides, he was struggling under his many layered
coat, it was starting to mat, and I was struggling to
keep up with the brushing. They say he wagged his
tail the entire time they buzzed off all the hair.

When I asked if the groomer had an opinion on his
particular ancestral cocktail, she laughed and said
"All twelve of them? He has at least twelve different
types of coat in there!" I know, I said. And they all
shed at the same time. Which is - all the time, as
copious hairballs flitting about the house could attest
to. Five minutes after a thorough vacuuming, there
they'd be, teasing and tickling. And even straight
from the groomers with his perky little scarf, he
managed to look scruffy. (That is, until he started
getting buzz cuts).

It's fun telling all these little stories, remembering my little shadow of over sixteen years. But then I remember what it means and my stomach plummets into deep, dark recesses. But that is all we who are left behind can do, isn't it? Remember and relish the memories of those who touched our hearts and souls beyond words, be they two or four-legged...

I feel like an amputee searching for a missing limb. Oh, Chico Man. You were with me for the better part of my adult life. I grew up with you. Now, you are here but not there. You are gone, but you have not left.

So I will remember you, Chico. I will remember your beautiful amber eyes and friendly smile. The way you picked me and never let go (unless treats were in the offering, then you became any man's best new friend for the duration), the funny trot and bouncing run and the way you'd sit and rise up, to go all melty and soft eyed when I rubbed your paws. Which was pretty much anytime you asked, how could I resist? Even if it was in the middle of teaching a lesson...

I will remember you as a cheerful puppy bumbling through a field of blue bonnets and trotting beside my horse, your matched white paws striding out with alacrity. I have memorized every hair on your brindle ears in your white face, your glistening black nose and the comical sight of the perfect white tip on your tail waving above golden grasses like the flag of a ship on high seas.

I will remember how you'd gently bump my leg for attention, and how it felt to hold your silky head and kiss you softly in the little hollow between your eyes and how you'd lean into the kiss, ever so slightly, then pull away like, yeah, yeah, enough, woman! I will never forget the warm affection you saved just for me, the special look you'd throw my way when you knew I was paying attention, the way your eyes would squint for a second as if you were winking at me with both eyes. I will laugh at how extra funny you were when hit by bouts of playfulness, all decorum and gentlemanly demeanour put aside for leaps, bounds and excited barking.

And how you'd do anything for a treat. After learning five tricks you'd try to do them all at once, perhaps thinking then you'd get all the treats at once, too.

I will remember your quiet dignity that lasted till the very end. I will remember how you slowly and quietly let me know it was time, and the gentle breeze that ruffled your many coats as I carried you to the shade of the oak tree my mother planted just after we moved here, ten years ago. I like to think she was there to greet you when you relinquished your tired old body. I will remember how, for the first time ever, you, a dog who hated to be held and carried, simply lay softly in my arms and rested your head on my shoulder as I hugged you closer and closer, desperate to not let go, though I knew I must.

And I will never forget how you took one final, long hard look around, then looked me full in the face for a long, long moment of silent communication, your beautiful soul shining through your eyes, so warm and present for the first time in days, beaming at me one last glorious shot of pure affection. I felt your love for me then as I felt mine for you, and I knew then as I have always believed, that there is more, much more, to a dog than so many will allow, as there is so much more to every sentient being on this earth than mankind will admit.

At the end, words failed me and I can't remember the many blessings and prayers of gratitude that poured from my heart but never passed my lips as the final injection was administered. Even now, I feel like I fail to do Chico justice. He touched the heart of everyone he met. He touched them and somehow, challenged their perception of 'it's just a dog'. Chico was never, ever - just a dog.

Perhaps no one has described Chico better than my close friend Jennifer, who wrote:

Here's to you, Chico!

You returned Love with Joy. Your perky trot and upright tail will never be forgotten, you jaunty gentleman! Thank you for the laughter and comfort you brought to all who knew you.

Hear, hear, Chico, and may you find a limitless supply of treats in Heaven and may all your tricks be rewarded tenfold.

So long, old friend, so long. I'll be seeing you.

The Little Book of Scattered Thoughts

Mixed Blessing

Last night, we had one of those incredible thunderstorms wash over us, the kind that Texas and Oklahoma are famous for. The kind that births tornadoes.

We desperately needed the rain and all day that is what I asked for. Rain but no tornadoes, please. Dear God, no tornadoes.

I got my wish but elsewhere, less than two hours from here, they were not so lucky. Six confirmed dead, dozens injured, hundreds homeless. This morning as I look with gratitude at my soaked garden and pastures, the flowers bright and happy after a long drink, the yellowing grass already green as Ireland again, others are sifting through broken belongings, looking at the iron sky through roofless homes and shattered windows, stumbling over splintered walls in shock and disbelief.

I've always loved thunderstorms. The electricity in the air, the blustering winds, the pelting rain, the booming and rolling of thunder and the blinding flashes of jagged light. It made me feel alive, the furore of Nature. It made feel like I was on fire with some unnamed desire and I should be standing on a towering ledge and scream with ferocity as the storm came galloping on hooves of thunder, whipped by hail.

Now I sit in prayer and scour the horizon with every flash of light that illuminates the darkness. Scour the horizon for any crooked fingers reaching down for the earth, twisting and jabbing at tender, vulnerable spots. Wonder if I should keep the horses in or out, what is safer? A roof over their heads against the stinging hail or worse - the deadly strike of a lightning bolt? Or the freedom to run should a tornado hit? Our storm shelter, after all, is only just big enough for us and five dogs.............

I know it's just the way of nature. I know it's part and parcel of life around here. But some days it makes me wonder. Some days, I miss getting to simply sit and enjoy a fine thunderstorm.

Passion Projects

Do you have a Passion project? If not, you should like, totally, like, you know, get one. Actually, you don't *get* a Passion Project. They get *you*. You don't even know you are getting gotten, you are just sitting quietly, drinking it all in, but when you get up - you are a changed person.

They get you and you get sleepless nights, early mornings, late nights, working all hours around your other life, worrying about money not just for your regular bills but for the project because the project MUST go on. You get hours of complete despondency because it all seems like it's going nowhere, a pipe dream, a storm in a glass of water, a sandcastle in the sky, a great mirage of wavering illusions.

You get to meet people who think you are nuts, ridiculous, people who stare at you blankly and ask Why? Why is that important? Why should that matter to me? You get to learn when to speak and when to simply shrug and say with a smile "If you have to ask why, I can't explain it to you."

You get to worry about letting down the people who have helped you get this far and you get to question your own sanity - repeatedly. You get to wonder what the heck you have gotten yourself into and *What on earth was I thinking??????*

Buuuuut you also get the overwhelming joy of feeling alive in the world, involved, inspired, enthusiastic, purpose-driven, the elation when you finally break through a wall and reach the next stage, the pride of having hung in there, made it happen, risked it all and lived to tell the story. You get to feel touched by the extraordinary, free of the mundane.

You get to meet wonderful people who run on parallel paths and offer spontaneous gestures of generosity. People who think you rock, who believe in you, in your vision, people who ask if they can help, people who put their hands in their pockets and pull out what they can to help you reach your goals. People who say that though they don't know you, they trust you, are proud of you and what you are becoming.

You get to grow as a human being, expand, become better acquainted with who you really are, or think you are, you get to peel layers off of your inner onion and discover just how much you believe - in your project, in your partners, in yourself, in your ability to go after something and manifest your dreams into your current reality.

You get to dream, a passionate and vibrant dream where your life will be one you can look back upon with pride and satisfaction. Not because you changed the world, but because you relinquished the safety of inertia and allowed the world to change you and the ripples of that change made a difference. Even if just to you.

Because when you change, the world changes.

A little over a year ago I went on a ride, on a lark, never suspecting it would turn me upside down, inside out. I wonder now how many lives Offbeat Safaris have changed simply by being who they are. How many lives can I change simply by being who I am? How many lives can you change simply by being who YOU are? Who is your most deep down Self, and what matters to that Self?

That is the question my Passion Project keeps asking me. To be me. The best of me, the most inspired, sincere, authentic, powerful, courageous...me. To not second guess, to not waiver, to not doubt that I am exactly what I am supposed to be, and that who I am is good enough to matter - when I dare to put all my talents to work.

<u>Big Life</u>

Whenever life gets me down

Like it did this morning

Met by the news that even three rhinos dehorned for
their safety

were not safe...

When I remember the numbers by which our big
life wildlife

are being decimated while the parties responsible....

deny, deny, deny..........

while the bullets fly

and our ellies and rhinos and lions and cheetahs and
gorillas and tigers and whales and sharks and, and,
and

are being pushed towards extinction

Ten years they say.

Ten years and we will see them only behind bars, the
ellies, the rhinos, the tigers...

And what little is left of the wilderness will be empty.

Susannah Cord

Ten years...

the last ten flew by.

So close, it's so close.

Then I remember all the incredible, dedicated,
tireless, brave, and inspiring people out there

who are fighting this good fight on the battlefield
itself.

People like Richard Bonham and his peers at the

Big Life Foundation.

The Glittering Sea

Some days, I miss the ocean. I do after all, descend from a nation of ocean-faring Vikings, and I did spend my early years in a kingdom of islands, surrounded by glittering seas. Never mind I did not inherit the unrockable bellies of the stalwart Vikings (and my father) and spent many a sailing vacation belly up and heaving over the side. That is beside the point.

The point is, now I live in a state of landlock, five-hundred miles from the ocean, five-hundred feet from a little pond that some days takes on the glittering aspect of my beloved sea. If I squint my eyes just so I can leave out the edges and the woods behind it. If I drive down the road I come across an enormous man-made dam and if I drive to just the right spot I come across a place where I can barely see the other shore and I can pretend it's a far more vast body of water than it is. Sometimes I place circling seagulls in the sky and flocks of dozens of gleaming, majestic, gliding white swans on the waters, just as I would see them in my home country.

Sometimes, like today, the sky above me reminds me of the sky above the sea on a Danish spring day.

Tempestuous, roiling, bright blue slipping behind clouds that promise rain but scurry on to sprinkle elsewhere, leaving the sun to peek promisingly through the fleeting gaps then shining on sudden showers of sparkling raindrops, falling gently and lightly on the upturned faces of man, beast and flower alike.

But the scent is all wrong. There is no damp and salty whiff to brace my lungs. My skin doesn't feel the humidity of a moisture laden air and when I breathe deeply it is not tangy with the potent smell of seaweed. I do not hear the crashing of surf on rocky shores, not even the gentle lapping of waves washing over sandy beaches and tempting me with their aquamarine promises of temperate waters when in fact, they will chill me to the bone in five seconds flat. My Viking blood too thinned by far......but not so far I am not still stirred with wanderlust and a longing for the unknown when faced with a large body of water.

Some days, I imagine the bottom of our hill ends not in a valley but the seaside, and my view from my window is not that of treetops but that of an endless expanse of a calmly rippling sea. I imagine I can hear seagulls crying their melancholic song, and the honking of swans. I have a little boat that I take out on quiet days when the equilibrium of my sensitive stomach will not be challenged and the wind is a gentle breeze that caresses my skin and my sails while the water laps and gurgles at my bow.

My Viking blood has been much thinned and my longing for the ocean is but a whisper of the call that once stirred my ancestors into extraordinary ocean-faring voyages. But it's still there, enough to turn my face to the East and feel the wind come calling, filling imaginary sails. Not complete and not fully fledged, no. I'm just a Mini-Viking, I guess.

Susannah Cord

Dream Big, Fly High

Been a very hectic week, with houseguests, clinics (that is when my mentor comes and works with me and my horses and my students and we all get our booties and brains worked off) and this Saturday, a birthday party for my husband. So much planning to do, and I've been neglecting my blog, I'm sorry to say. But never mind finding Time - finding *Mind* was all but impossible.

At the same time, a wonderful opportunity may have come along to do something I have never done before, something that would challenge me in new ways and yet something I can't help but feel I could do and do well. Almost like I've just been waiting and preparing for it to come along. So my brain has been galloping along on multiple tracks at top speeds.....

But last night I had the most wonderful dream that I had to tell you about while it's still fresh in my mind and its emotional footprint still clear on my heart.

I dreamt I could fly. I often have those dreams, and sometimes it's easy and sometimes it's hard, but it's always very real. I am not a bird or a plane, I don't have wings or engines - I fly on the wings and power of Spirit. I simply lift myself into the air and off I go, fuelled by intention.

Last night I flew the best I ever have. It was easy, I was agile, light and confident. I swooped and dove and laughed my way across the heavens. I swept across a glittering sea where Tall Ships swayed majestically with billowing sails. I rolled on my back and floated with arms outstretched and hands open to the blue, blue sky.

When I landed, I was in a room full of people. They asked me why I was so happy. I told them it was because I could fly. They looked at me strangely and said not a thing. I knew I was going out on a limb telling these strangers something so wild and wonderful about myself and that they probably would not believe me, but still, I would not recant.

"I can fly!" I said happily. "And you know," I carried on, "The thing is, I think everyone can. They have just forgotten how." And as I said it, I knew it was true and I wished fervently that everyone in that room would remember.

That is where the dream ended and I woke up in bliss. I got up and opened a book to a random page and this is what it said:

The Little Book of Scattered Thoughts

"Don't just see the magic, engage it! Challenge it! Dare it! Dream big,

with every expectation that your dreams will manifest.

Demand that they come true! You're not beholden to life. Life is beholden to you.

You are its reason for being. You came first."

Notes from the Universe by Mike Dooley

I think it's telling me it's time to spread my wings. What's it telling you?

Susannah Cord

Choice. Chance. Change

Look before you leap. Don't fly higher than your wings can carry. When in doubt, don't. And don't burn your bridges!

Sage advice we all have heard, many a time. But is it always right? What happens when it leaves you petrified? Life stops, you stop, growth stops. Everything gets smaller, tighter, contracted, boring. Depressing.

There's a reason perfectly sane people suddenly break out and seek the rush of adrenalin, whether in a mad leap into craggy canyons when bungie jumping, shooting and snorting up drugs, driving too fast on narrow roads with hairpin turns. Because taking a chance - and surviving it - makes us feel good, exhilarated, powerful.

Alive.

I saw this on Facebook the other day:

"Choice"
"Chance"
"Change"

You Must Make A "Choice"
To Take A "Chance"
Or
Your Life Will Never "Change"

It made me stop and think. I have taken a lot of Chances in my life. I have made a lot of Choices, some that made friends and family question my sanity, to the point a few declared they could not respect the choices I was making and turned their backs on me for a time. Still, I carried on down my path. Because I had to. I was compelled by some inner conviction. Was it fun? Was it easy? Was it joyful? No.

It was Change.

Fun, easy and joyful came later.

I made the choices that I had to, the choices that called me, the choices that fit me. Not everyone else, or what they thought I should do to be a decent, perfect, exemplary, civilized human being. Sometimes it took courage, sometimes it took heart, sometimes it took a massive leap of faith.

Always it took a Choice.

When people ask me about my life they often exclaim how interesting and exciting and lucky my life has been. Yes, it has. I have been lucky, but I have also been the maker of Choices, the taker of Chancers and the seeker of Change, the Captain of my life to the degree that I could fathom at the time. Which often times, was not much. Not much at all. I only knew that Life could not bring me a new day untill I left the old one behind. Sometimes, you gotta burn a bridge. Or two. You gotta leap without looking, knowing full well there is no safety net in the traditional sense of the word. You have to crack your life wide open so you can let Luck in.

It's also been a lot of work, fears, tears, doubts and second guessing. There have been lots of what ifs, what nows, and what fors. Long hours and longer days.

But sometimes, when life closes in, you can't take it anymore and you stand at the fork in the road, bewildered because nothing is clear, obvious, all is shrouded in fog.......that is when you have to make a Choice, take that Chance if you want things to Change. It is a choice made in the heart and when all the voices around you and in your head have had their say, there is only one voice left that counts.

That is when I close my eyes and listen to the teeny, tiny tug on my heart that tells me where to turn. And then I leap. I don't even look first. After all, once my heart has spoken, I am no longer in doubt my wings will carry me every bit as high as they need to.

Gratitude

Gratitude. It's the stuff of life. The feel good stuff. It's the conduit between praying and receiving, it's the warm glow and the bubbling joy. It's good to remember - and a little bit will go a long, long way.

My mother - who would have been seventy-three today, Happy Birthday, Mom! - used to tell me to Count My Blessings. As a child I didn't quite understand - with a child's Faith that all will always be well, I took it all for granted. As a teenager, I resented it. I felt like she was telling me I didn't really deserve my good fortune. As a young adult, I didn't know how I could possibly feel gratitude when life was so very, very hard.

But little by little, it began to dawn on me. Little by little, I learned to become grateful for even the littlest things. I began, after all, to Count My Blessings. And when I did, I discovered a very odd thing about myself.

Somewhere along the way, I had come to fear feeling gratitude. Somehow, feeling gratitude had become linked to a sense of unworthiness, that if I felt grateful for something it must be because I had received something I did not deserve. If I acknowledged my good fortune, perhaps it would be ripped from me. Yes, God's ways may be mysterious but the Mind comes a close second.

So practicing gratitude became an exercise in self-worth. Funny how things turn out. The more gratitude I felt, the more I got to acknowledge my own self-worth. All of a sudden, when I felt gratitude I also had an opportunity to feel it as an acknowledgement of my own worthiness in receiving. It's a win-win! It's also a little bit of work, still. I have to remind myself I am not just blessed - I am worthy of my blessings.

Why? Because I am a child of God and worth it, that's why!!! Just ask L'Oreal.

Blessings come in all sizes. Yesterday I received a package I was not expecting. I opened it with a puzzled frown on my face. It was a thoughtful gift from a new friend and my heart opened like a red rose in bloom. I was overwhelmed by her generosity and thoughtfulness. My frown turned upside down and became a deeply touched smile. It fuelled the rest of my day.

Blessings can be self-prescribed. In the morning I am met by a million sights for which to be grateful – five waggy dogs, four nickering horses, three braying donkeys, two miaowing cats, one rising sun, acres of serene pastureland, dozens of singing birds, a sleepy husband, a steaming cup of my favourite tea, and a partridge in a pear tree....and the ability and time to enjoy it all.

Blessings can be acts of God. Like my mother, who while being the greatest blessing of all, taught me to Count My Blessings. Nobody loves you like your Mama, nobody forgives like your Mama, nobody knows you like your Mama, and nobody infuriates you like your Mama. It is said you don't know what you've got till it's gone, and that is partly true. It is also true that for every time she drove me mad, there were a hundred for which I simply sat and gave thanks for having a wonderful mother. A fiercely loyal, devoted, supportive, adoring, always forgiving and welcoming me home, mother.

So while I now miss coming home to my mother and instead tend a grave, I am just grateful I ever had her at all. And that, my friends, is a blessing to be counted, Always and Forever.